# BADA$$ BUSINESS WRITING

# BADA$$ BUSINESS WRITING

## 5 Illustrated Lessons for Better Communication at Work

**Jenny Morse, PhD.**
**& John Garvey**

Bada$$ Business Writing: 5 Illustrated Lessons for Better Communication at Work
Published by Jargon's Nerve Publishing, LLC
Fort Collins, Colorado, U.S.A.



MORSE, JENNY, and GARVEY, JOHN, Authors
BADA$$ BUSINESS WRITING
JENNY MORSE and JOHN GARVEY

ISBN: 978-0-578-39992-8 (digital)
979-8-9872116-0-1 (paperback)

HUMOR / Topic / Business & Professional
BUSINESS & ECONOMICS / Business Writing
LANGUAGE ARTS & DISCIPLINES / Writing / Business Aspects

Editing & Book Design: Michelle M. White (MMWBooks.com)
Publishing Consultant: Susie Schaefer (FinishTheBookPublishing.com)

# TABLE OF CONTENTS

## CHAPTER 3
## EDITING
### *Tools Any Knucklehead Can Use*
23



## CHAPTER 4
## GRAMMAR
### *It's Not Just for Fascists*
29

CHAPTER 5

## BE NICE

*But Don't Be a Wuss*

53



CONCLUSION

*You Eloquent Bastard*

65

APPENDIX

*Resources*

67

ABOUT THE AUTHORS

*John Garvey & Jenny Morse*

69

INTRODUCTION

# WRITING WELL IN ENGLISH

## *Why Should You Care?*

When you were growing up, you learned a dizzying number of rules. Some seemed stupid at the time, but you recognize as an adult that they were sensible. Others are still stupid. You probably feel this way about a lot of grammatical rules that supposedly apply to you.

We have some good news for you. In many cases, you're right: Those are stupid rules. You can break them, and nothing will happen.

Serious-minded businesspeople don't care if you say "may" when "might" would have been correct. They don't care if you start a sentence with "And" or end it with a preposition. When dealing with writing, they care about two things:

1. You respect their time—your writing gets to the point.
2. You are clear—they understand what you are saying and what's expected of them. They don't have to re-read, search the message for the "so what," psychoanalyze your tone, or google vocabulary words every time you email them.

## THE PARADOX OF BUSINESS WRITING

If you write clearly enough for a 9-year-old to understand, you'll sound intelligent.

Should you strive to intimate your intelligence in your manuscripts, you'll appear obtuse.
(***Translation***: If you try to sound smart, you'll end up sounding stupid.)

If writing is both an art and a science, we're looking at it mostly as a science. In other words, there's solid data backing most of the lessons that follow. Those lessons will help you be a happier, more effective, and more empowered professional. They'll save you time. They'll save your colleagues time. They'll make you more persuasive.

Specifically, here's how the lessons in this guide will benefit you:

- You'll get better responses to your emails.
- You'll spend less time answering questions because people will understand what you mean the first time you say it.
- You'll come across as more approachable.
- You'll come across as more competent.
- You'll spend less time banging your head against your keyboard because you'll have a clearer sense of what merits your attention.

We're not handing you a license to write like a 9-year-old. We're just clarifying what's actually useful for professionals. Flowery writing is stupid. Making someone look up definitions in order to understand a written request is annoying. Phrasing a statement as a question makes you sound like someone who might accidentally put his socks on over his shoes. Your coworkers don't want to read anything you write anyway. Don't make it harder for them!

"DAMMIT, I KNEW ALL THOSE POINTLESSLY LONG-WINDED EMAILS WOULD EVENTUALLY KILL US ALL."

Basically, your writing should

1. Be brief
2. Use proper email etiquette
3. Be edited
4. Use good grammar
5. Be nice

And if that's too much, focus on #1 and #5.

The rest of the book will explore each of these points in greater detail, so forge on to find out what you may be doing wrong and how you can write better.

# CHAPTER 1

# BREVITY

## Short is Better than Long (in Writing)

One of the most frustrating things about being human is . . .

Um, what was I about to say? . . .

Oh, yeah: **Forgetfulness**.

Never underestimate how forgetful and distracted someone might be at any given time. If you're able to get someone's attention in the first place, it's safe to say they already have at least three or four other things on their mind: an email they need to respond to, a conversation they're dwelling on, their kid's test scores, or an upcoming social commitment.

While they are reading whatever it is you've written, they can and do look away from it—regularly. They do not read all of your carefully crafted words. So, choose the words you write and send only the most important ones.

Brevity doesn't always mean ultra-short writing. It means not using two words where one will do. Simplify. The simpler and briefer you are, the more likely your reader will understand (and remember) your message.

Here are some quick and easy tips to put this principle to use:

1. Proofread every email before you send it and try to shorten it by at least one sentence.
1. If the last line of a paragraph is just a few words, cut words out of the paragraph until the last line disappears.
2. Look for repeated words or ideas and delete them.
3. Stop using lengthy phrases:

- due to the fact = because
- with regards to = about
- of superb quality = superb
- provide stability = stabilize
- possess the ability to = can
- in this manner = this way

Lists of these phrases exist. They're useful!

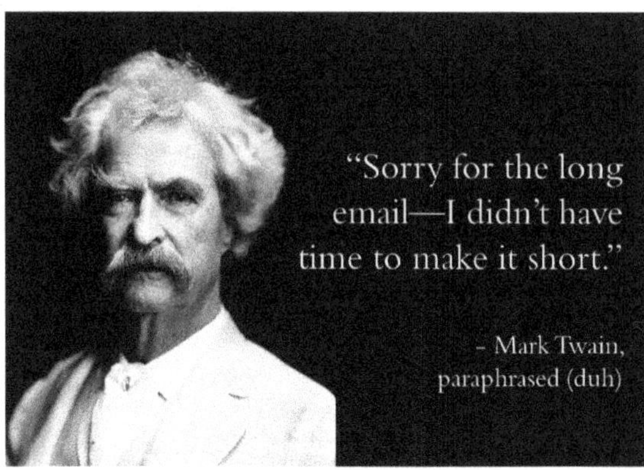

CHAPTER 2

# PROPER ETIQUETTE FOR EMAIL

## *Because People Like Easy*

Email is the most used form of writing in the business world today. Business writers send and receive 121 emails per day on average, according to Campaign Monitor. That's a lot of email.

By following our guidelines, you should be able to reduce that. Write better messages, decrease the number of back-and-forth email exchanges, and increase the likelihood stuff gets done right the first time. Here are the key parts to focus on: the subject line, the greeting, the closing, the timing, the paragraphing, and the ask.

## SUBJECT LINES

The subject line is the first part of your message a person reads. We use the subject to find out what the email is about and to decide whether to open it—or not.

If you want your recipient to open your email, make sure you include information relevant to them. Simply writing "Question" in the subject line is not helpful. Neither is writing to a banker with the subject "Account." Or writing to a prospective client about a vague "Meeting." The more specific your subject line is, the more likely you are to get a useful response.

These questions should guide the development of your subject line:

- What do you want the other person to do?
- About what?
- By when?

Here are some examples of issues and effective subject lines:

Sofia needs IT to help her record a presentation for Kronos, a prospective client, on Monday.

**Subject:** Record Kronos presentation on Monday 7/12

> Ian needs to get a plaque for the Founders Award by Friday.
> **Subject:** Create Founders Award plaque by Friday 9/2
>
> Eli of Pay Corp wants to meet with Danielle of Media Inc to discuss a partnership between their two companies.
> **Subject:** Pay Corp and Media Inc partnership meeting

Consider that it feels much nicer to include a deadline in the subject line rather than flag a message as urgent. If you tell the audience in the subject line when something needs to be done, you are providing practical information. If you flag something, you are telling them what you need done is more important than whatever they are working on. Telling other people what to do with their time is rude.

Keep your subject lines short and specific, and include any relevant details about timing.

## GREETINGS

Business culture may be less formal now than 20 years ago, but salutations still matter. How you start your message sets the tone for what follows. And since most writing will never sound as nice as anything you can say out loud, you're already starting from a deficit. Make sure your greeting is nice! Greetings received well have two parts: a greeting word or phrase like "Hi" and the person or group's name.

From formal to informal, greetings go like this:

**Dear Ms. Smith:**
greeting word = dear, name = title and last name, colon = stay away

**Dear Ms. Smith,**
comma = one-armed hug

**Good morning, Ms. Smith,**
greeting phrase = good afternoon/good morning

> Notice the presence of *two* commas: the phrase "good afternoon" is something you are saying *to* Ms. Smith. This comma is important. Without it, you may inadvertently insult people or make fun of them. For example,
>
> **Good morning staff**
> is a dirty joke; whereas
>
> **Good morning, staff,**
> is a pleasant greeting to your employees.

**Dear Emily Smith,**
**Good morning, Emily Smith,**
name = first and last

**Dear Emily,**
**Good afternoon, Emily,**
**Hi Emily,**
name = first

Currently, *hey* and other alternatives to *hi* are not considered "professional." That doesn't mean you can't use them; it just means you should feel very comfortable with people when you use them.

Most of us will probably use the last example in this list as our primary greeting. Remember, "Dear" is formal standard, meaning it is appropriate in formal contexts where you do not have— nor do you intend to have—a personal relationship with the other person/business, like writing to a bank, a utility company, or a potential employer.

On the other end of formality, you don't have to use a greeting on every message when you are responding to an email thread.

## CLOSINGS

The closing is the final word before your name at the end of the message. It is essential that you have a closing, as it marks the end of the message and lets the reader know they have received your complete thoughts. But it is not important *what* it is. Closings are meant to convey some sense of how you feel about the message or the other person, which is why—

> Sincerely,

and

> Respectfully,

—are considered standard formal closings. You put the closing word or phrase, a comma, a return, and then your first name or signature block:

Sincerely,
The Authors

Other options are the following:

Regards
Best regards
Kind regards
Warm regards
Best
Kindly
Warmly
Cheers
Aloha

Many people choose to end with "Thank you" or "Thanks," but use these with caution. Thanking people *before* they do something can feel rude or uncomfortable. When you thank beforehand, you are indicating that you expect them to complete the requested action—much like the incredibly presumptuous phrase "Thank you in advance." Save your gratitude for after they have fulfilled your request, so you can mean it.

If you feel compelled to use "Thanks" as your closing, please thank people for something specific. Thank them for helping you out. Thank them for making your job easier. Thank them for adhering to the schedule. Your open-ended gratitude is a waste and makes you sound less grateful every time you use it.

Choose a word or phrase you are comfortable putting at the end of most emails and stick with it. You can always switch to "Thank you" for those specific messages where you are showing gratitude.

## TIMING

Don't contribute to the stress of our "always on, always accountable" culture. Leave people alone during odd hours and on weekends unless you can confidently say it's okay (or necessary) given the specific situation or your relationship. If you have an email you want to get out of the way, you can easily schedule it to go out at a later time.

Standard response time for an email is 24 hours during the week. If you need a response sooner, don't be a dick about it.

*Is managing your inbox not a pain in the ass?!?* Assume the person you're writing to has it as least as bad as you do and give them a little grace. Never take it personally if you don't get a response within 48 hours of sending an email.

If your message really needs a response sooner, consider calling or texting.

Be careful about using flags or other markers of your own urgency. Using flags is weirdly more annoying than using "URGENT" or "PLEASE RESPOND" in the subject line. And all caps is really freakin' annoying. What is urgent and important to you may not be urgent or important to me.

(EMAIL MARKED AS "URGENT")

Put the deadline in the subject line. Allow others to figure out from that how to organize and prioritize their time. And remember, if you use "ASAP" too many times, you are just asking for a wolf to come and gobble up all of your sheep.

## PARAGRAPHING

Paragraphs exist to signal to the reader a change in the main idea. New paragraph, new idea.

You don't need to indent new paragraphs with email. Use a white space between paragraphs instead. The white space between paragraphs is a stronger visual marker to show that an email contains multiple ideas and that the employee, who doesn't *want* to read the email, at least needs to look at the 2 or 3 or 4 paragraphs to complete the task.

Most people will at least look at the first half of the first line of each paragraph, even if they don't want to read the whole message. So, put important information there.

And make sure the paragraphs are short enough that the reader can easily see the end of them. We are less likely to read a paragraph if we can't see where it ends—TL; DR (that's "Too Long; Didn't Read").

Finally, short paragraphs show that you are thinking about how your audience reads. When the reader sees signs that you have thought about them in advance, they're more inclined to like you and want to read more. It's basic respect.

## A CLEAR "ASK"

Since we write emails from the privacy of our own computers, out of sight of their intended audiences, we sometimes feel like we can just start writing and "see where it goes." Send it, and let the other person figure out what the central message is. But when you create more work for someone else, you are less likely to get your audience to do *anything*.

Make it incredibly easy for your recipients to act. Whether you're responding or initiating a conversation (assuming you have any sense of purpose whatsoever), it's almost always because you want something. Even if you're writing to offer someone help, or reconnecting with a friend, surely there's something you want to know. Don't make them piece it together. Ask.

How will you do that? By stating or asking—clearly—what you want them to do. At least 19 out of 20 good emails contain a question.

Where will you put this request? In the first sentence or the last paragraph. Most good messages begin or end with a question.

Why there? Because those are the two places where most of your readers will look (see Paragraphing above).

Think about it. If you want your partner to do the dishes, and they never, ever do the dishes, you don't put a note asking them to do the dishes next to the dishes. You put a note asking them to do the dishes on the back of the toilet or on the inside of the front door or on their phone. You put it where they are likely to look. Do the same thing in your emails.

In framing the request, you can make it a statement or a question. Questions tend to work better because a request not framed as a question will either sound bossy, vague, or wimpy.

Let's say you have a client who is relocating, and you want to hand their account to a client management specialist at another office closer to the client's new location. So, you write to your colleague telling them all about your client. And you need to know when your colleague wants the client's files transferred over. You can phrase this request in the following ways, organized from least nice to most nice:

> I'll transfer the client files to you this Friday.
>
> Let me know when you want me to transfer the client files to you.

Please let me know when you want me to transfer the client files to you.

When would you like me to transfer the client files to you?

Any one of these 4 sentences clearly states the request, but they each have a different impact on the audience. The first one says *you don't have a choice. I'm doing this whether you like it or not.* And sometimes you will be in the position to do or say that to your audience. But recognize that it is not nice.

The second one is completely neutral. Like an awkward wallflower at a high school dance, it is likely to be passed over.

The third one is just slightly nicer than the second because it uses *please*. This one shows you have good manners. But since it lacks a question mark, you might not get a response. You might be left in limbo, wondering when you should send the files, or if your colleague even got the email.

The fourth one is the best because it's both a clear request and an invitation. It invites the other person to decide when they want the files. It has the additional advantage of using a question mark so the reader knows that they need to write you back, that you are waiting for their response.

Asking questions isn't just about manners. It's about communicating needs and expectations so you'll get what you want.

CHAPTER 3

# EDITING

## *Tools Any Knucklehead Can Use*

(Disclaimer: No tool fixes everything.)

You must edit your work. Or you must get someone else to edit it. Please do not send messages that you have not reviewed. People hate that. And they will laugh at you.

If you don't feel up to the task, you'll find some recommended services below. If you are confident in your competence, the On Your Own section of this chapter offers some suggestions to help you be a better proofreader. Please consider doing both: review your writing yourself *and* use a service. People will appreciate you.

## SERVICES

1. Grammarly – grammarly.com – It's only a modest exaggeration to say we dread the thought of sending an email without Grammarly switched on. Grammarly catches most misspellings and misconjugations. It's not perfect, though. It's run by bots.
2. Hemingway – hemingwayapp.com – Another free tool, Hemingway helps you flag sentences that are hard to read or obnoxious in minor ways seasoned professionals tend not to notice. It flags excessive use of adverbs ("generally," "slightly," "obviously," etc.), passive voice, and pointlessly complex language.
3. Boomerang – boomeranggmail.com – Never again forget to follow up on an important email that goes unanswered. Boomerang lets you schedule emails you send to return to your inbox if unanswered. It also gives a loose assessment about how cordial your email is, how direct, and (usual disclaimers aside) the likelihood that you'll get a response.

Boomerang also lets you schedule outgoing emails to send at a time of your choosing, so people don't realize what a psycho you are writing emails at 2:07 in the morning.

Psycho.

CAVEAT: These tools are all based on algorithms. They use rules that are generally correct, but they aren't sophisticated enough to recognize where exceptions apply.

Even Microsoft Word spellcheck and grammar check, which have been around forever, are unreliable. Someone threw a grammar book at a bunch of computer programmers and told them to build grammar check. So, they built a program that's rigidly opinionated and yet often wrong. Language has rules, but all of them, every single one, can be legally and responsibly broken. The computer programmers only programmed the rules, not the infinite legit exceptions.

Plus, rules change.

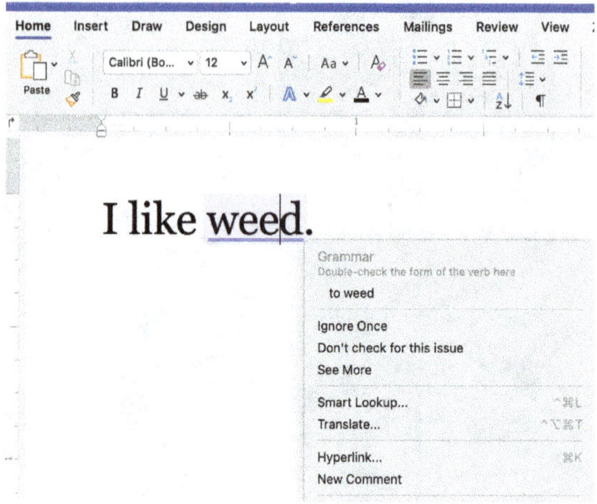


***This is the reason Microsoft doesn't get to hang with the FAANG companies.***

So, when these tools flag things in your writing, think of them as nudges, not directives. They are very good at drawing your attention to potential errors, and they'll help you recognize tendencies that make your writing mentally taxing to readers. But they're bots. (Don't forget *The Terminator*. Things can get really out of hand when bots start running the show.)

Be the human who keeps the bots in line.

## ON YOUR OWN

If you choose to proofread your work yourself (you brave soul, you), here are some things you should do if you want to be successful. The bots may not be perfect, but—and we hate to break this to you—neither are you (at proofreading).

1. Wait 15 minutes until you forget what you wrote, then read it again.
2. Read out loud.
3. Touch the page/screen with your finger as you read.
4. Kill trees. As odd as it might sound, you'll notice things you overlooked on a screen when you proofread a printed document.
5. Change fonts. Somewhat like printing, changing fonts tricks part of your brain into thinking it's seeing something new. The novelty gives you greater attention to detail. The font *Barlow* is lovely.
6. Cover the page/screen to show only one line at a time.
7. Start with the last sentence and read backwards.
8. Get another brain (a friend's—don't take their brain, just ask to borrow it. We're not zombies here).

CHAPTER 4

# GRAMMAR

## *It's Not Just for Fascists*

Here's our take on grammar: The rules don't matter because of the rules themselves. The rules matter for 2 reasons:

1. Understanding. If we don't follow most of the same rules, you can't understand me. Here is the same sentence out of order: Rules me follow can't of you understand same we if don't most the. Grammar does matter. But "If we follow mosta the same rules you kin understand me" only breaks two rules—common spellings and a missing comma. You can still understand it.

Correctness = mutual understanding.

2. And credibility. We use correct grammar as a superficial way of deciding whether people we don't know can be trusted. Consider spam in email. A main way we recognize it is through grammar errors. For example, "Kindly revert back if you have projects that needs funding for further discussion and negotiation." Revert: did they mean reply? Projects that needs: typo or English is not their first language? Grammar errors suggest either carelessness—a person didn't take time to review their work, so that person doesn't care about us—or incompetence—a person doesn't know enough grammar to be able to communicate correctly, so that person probably doesn't know even more important things.

Correctness = instant credibility.

With those goals in mind, "Top 5 Stupid Grammar Rules You Still Have To Think About," on the next page, tells you what you should be doing, and "Top 5 Stupid Grammar Rules You Don't Have To Think About (Anymore)," on page 43, tells you what ridiculous rules your 6th grade teacher forced you to learn that you don't actually have to follow.

## TOP 5 STUPID GRAMMAR RULES YOU STILL HAVE TO THINK ABOUT

If you are trying to be understood and get people to trust you, these 5 grammar rules matter:

1. ***Oxford commas. Because shit happens when you don't keep your Oxford comma in plain sight.***

The Oxford comma, AKA the serial comma, is the name for the comma that appears right before the last item in a list.

> Today I have to go for a run, grade student papers, email my assistant, and finish reading my book.

That little comma highlighted in green? That's the Oxford comma. And a punctuation mark that's been the center of legendary debate.

Lucky for you, writer of American English, the debate has been at least temporarily settled. In 2014 a group of truckers in Maine sued their employer for overtime. Their contract said that they wouldn't be paid for doing a series of things:

> You will not be paid overtime for the canning, processing, preserving, freezing, drying, marketing, storing, packing for shipment or distribution of agricultural products.

Notice the yellow highlight: no comma.

So, do they get paid overtime for distributing the goods as long as they're not *packing* the goods? According to the courts, without the comma separating those two items, the contract was treating them as a unit. As long as they were simply distributing the agricultural goods, not packing them up, they got paid overtime. (This example is paraphrased and in no way illustrates the exact argument of the truckers or their employers.)

Put another way: If I ask you to do *a, b, and c,* I have asked you to do 3 things. If I ask you to do *a, b and c,* I may have asked you to do two things because b and c should be done together.

The truckers won the argument in court, and they won on two appeals.

Outcome: we should all be using the Oxford comma in our professional writing since it could potentially end up in court.

You are now a proud user of the Oxford comma! Congrats!

### 2. *Apostrophes. They are annoying, but English requires them.*

Lots of languages don't use apostrophes. For example, Swedish doesn't use them; neither does Spanish. In Spanish, you can't say "my friend's jacket." You have to say "the jacket of my friend." But in Swedish you can say "my friends jacket" just like you would in English but without the apostrophe! Mind blown.

Apostrophes in English have two purposes: elision and possession.

Elision means that something has been skipped over.

| Hasn't | Won't | Should've | '70s |
|---|---|---|---|

The words above use the apostrophe to show that we've skipped some letters, in full below.

| Has not | Will not | Should have | 1970s |
|---|---|---|---|

Possession means that something belongs to someone or something else.

My friend's jacket = the jacket belonging to my friend
1970s' fashion = fashion that belongs in the 1970s
Jim's car = the car belonging to Jim

We also have a bunch of pronouns in English that show possession and already include the idea conveyed by *'s*: *his, her/hers, their/theirs, its, your/yours, our/ours, my/mine*. Confusingly, some of these words sound a lot like other words that do use apostrophes: *they're, you're, it's*—but those words are contractions, which use the apostrophe to show elision.

The *'s* comes with several challenges. Many of these challenges can be resolved by asking yourself two questions before adding *'s*. First:

1. Do I have two nouns next to each other? Most people remember quite easily what a noun is (person, place, or thing) while they're unable to recall the definition of any other part of speech. Luckily, as long as you know what a noun is, you can determine if you have two nouns next to each other. If you do, chances are the first one is owning the second one. In that case, you want an apostrophe.

Now where do you put the apostrophe? That's where question 2 comes in:

2. Am I talking about one thing or many things? One thing that owns another thing gets *'s*: one company's car. If many things own the other thing, it's *s'*:

two companies' cars. (And note that if your first word doesn't end in *s*, you use *'s* just like before: women's cars.)

Hopefully, this sounds easy to you. Two nouns next to each other? Need an apostrophe. One thing? *'s*. Many things? *s'*.

That's a good start. But we wouldn't be talking about English if it were easy.

A common question occurring to some people right now is, "What if the one owner's name ends in *s*?" Ah, yes. So, if I'd used Travis as an example above instead of Jim, what happens with the car belonging to Travis?

Travis' car **or** Travis's car

Yes.

Grammar people have not decided which one is correct because both versions follow a certain kind of logic. Like the Oxford comma, you'll find people on both sides of this debate. And, unfortunately, there's no court case to turn to. Personally, I prefer Travis's car because when I speak, I make 2 *s* sounds. But both are considered correct, as long as you're consistent in your choice within the same document.

And now, with many people starting to realize that grammar is just a bunch of made-up rules, you might come to another question: "What about holiday cards?"

Ah, yes. First, if you are going to sign a holiday card, do you have two nouns next to each other? Is your family showing ownership of anything? No. So, you are unlikely to use an apostrophe.

> "Holiday greetings from the Smith's"

just leaves all kinds of questions open. The Smith's what? What thing that the friendly neighborhood blacksmith owns is sending me holiday greetings??

Second question: are you talking about one thing or many things? Presumably, you are talking about all the people in your family, which means you need to make your last name plural.

We form plurals for words that end with *s* and *s*-like sounds by adding es: bus/buses, Kleenex/Kleenexes, brush/brushes. This same rule applies if your last name ends in an *s* sound.

Let's say your name is Cordelia Matthews. You want to sign a card from the whole family. That card would be signed

> "From the Matthewses"

No joke.

And if you want to make a sign for your driveway to welcome people to your humble abode?

> "Welcome to The Matthewses' House"

Yes, you read that correctly. Your name would be plural with an *es* first and then an apostrophe after the *s* to show that the house belongs to you.

Often where apostrophes are misused, they're being used incorrectly on plurals. For example, real estate development signs:

> Houses from the low 300's.

No. There is no apostrophe on 300s. Because you are talking about a plural (multiple possible numbers) not a possessive. The 300s don't own anything. Go back to the two questions and try again.

My recommendation: don't use an apostrophe unless you're certain you need it. And when in doubt, just re-word what you were going to say. You can always just write "From the Matthews family" and avoid apostrophes, plurals, and the whole mess.

### 3. *Spelling. Because there's just one letter between assess and asses.*

For centuries, spelling was the most common "error" in writing. Various people and institutions tried to standardize spelling, but when all your books had to be written by hand and transported by donkey or boat, it was very difficult to standardize anything at all. Handwritten documents from different regions and people had all kinds of different versions of the same word.

Then, those handwritten documents got transcribed into printed ones and mass produced starting in the 15th century (Thanks, Gutenberg). People in northern England suddenly got loads of books from southern England and said, "wait a minute, they spell it like *that*?" and your Oxford-comma-level fisticuffs began. Then we started printing dictionaries, and suddenly everyone could be a great speller! Well, at least it was possible.

A few decades ago, along came spellcheck. Essentially, the dictionary is programmed into your computer and now it checks your words for you! Amazing! Except that English has a lot of words that aren't spelled the way they sound and words that sound like other words that are spelled differently (plus some of those regional people were very insistent on keeping their own spelling, so we actually have multiple acceptable spellings of words—grey or gray, for example). All spelling has to do with context.

Did you know that there are some languages where spelling is so closely related to the sound of the language that children can correctly spell every word in the language, even if they don't know what it means and have never heard it before? In these languages, a spelling bee like our Scripps event would be laughable because everyone would be a winner.

English is hard. And spelling matters.

Our masochistic culture takes great pleasure in deriding people for their misspellings, whether they are teeny accidental typos or clear signs that the person doesn't know what they're talking about. Either way, spelling in English is tied to credibility. Nothing so easily destroys our faith in each other as misspelled words. Let's not even mention covfefe.

Keep in mind that in order to benefit from spellcheck, you must be patient enough to let it do its work. Use the tool, check the tool, check your own writing. And memorize potential problems: their or thier?

## 4. *Homophones and word choice. You're welcome.*

Related to spelling is the issue of homophones. Homophones are words that sound the same but are spelled differently and have different meanings.

| | |
|---|---|
| capitol = building | capital = letter |
| desert = dry wasteland | dessert = sugary goodness |
| manner = way | manor = house |
| apart = separate | a part = included |

There are lists of these. Spellcheck cannot catch them all. You have to.

English is full of homophones: to, too, two. Why have we done this to ourselves? Unclear, but we are now responsible for using the language effectively by spelling the words that we mean the way they have to be spelled.

Or don't care about it and try not to care when people laugh at you and correct your writing.

### 5. *Lists & bullet points. AKA parallelism or parallel structure*

Say you're creating a presentation and on many slides you use bullet points. For example, one slide in your presentation says something like this:

These masks can be great for

- Hiking
- At school or work
- Trip to the grocery store

While we understand the ideas presented in the bullets, we've unfortunately run across a grammatical error: a lack of parallelism. The ideas in your list are not in the same grammatical form, which means they are not parallel. How do we know? Try to write each bullet point as its own sentence:

- These masks can be great for hiking. Check.
- These masks can be great for at school or work. Nope.

- These masks can be great for trip to the grocery store. Nope.

In order to make the list parallel (and thus grammatically correct), we have to change the information in the bullets so that each item fits in the same place in the sentence.

- These masks can be great for ~~at~~ school or work.
- These masks can be great for a trip to the grocery store.

Now, we rewrite our bullets:

These masks can be great for

- Hiking
- School or work
- A trip to the grocery store

Parallelism is important in sentences that don't have bullets, too. Any time you have a list, you need to check it.

Bullets, especially in presentations, tend to have this mistake a lot. And when we read these kinds of lists carefully, they make us feel icky. Please make sure to help your audiences feel good by aligning all of your bullets with the same root sentence.

## TOP 5 STUPID GRAMMAR RULES YOU DON'T HAVE TO THINK ABOUT (ANYMORE)

When you were learning to write, your teachers told you certain lies, well-intentioned lies, to help you become a solid writer. These lies are much like the lies our parents told us or you tell your kids as a shortcut because you don't want to explain your full reasoning. You might tell your children that the "playground is closed" when you don't want to take them. But then your 5-year-old starts saying places are closed when he doesn't want to go: "school is closed." You've accidentally taught him a "rule" that doesn't exist. Our English teachers did the same thing.

1. ***Beginnings. Yes, you can begin a sentence with And, But, or Because.***

The lie that you can't start a sentence with *and* or *but* or *because* is one that sticks with some people. Why did your teacher tell you this lie? Because your teacher wanted you to write complete sentences. You had to learn that a sentence needs a subject and a verb. And that a sentence expresses a complete idea. It's a lot easier to say "don't start a sentence with *and*" than to explain "your sentence isn't correct here because you don't have a subject and a verb."

But now that you know how sentences work, you can be trusted to write complete ones. Or to break the rules for emphasis and style, not from ignorance. Go ahead, start a sentence with *and, but, because, or,* and all those other words you were told not to use. We've done it here, and the world didn't end. You're an adult. You can write a complete sentence starting with any word you want. Almost.

2. ***Endings. Yes, you can end a sentence with a preposition.***

> *I asked this Northern woman, "Where are ya'll from?" And she said, 'I'm from a place where we don't end our sentences with prepositions.' So I said, "Okay, where are ya'll from, bitch?"*
>
> —Charlene, Designing Women

This lie was because grammar people like rules, and for some reason this rule, which has something to do with Latin grammar, became one that grammar people clung to. While Latin is one of the ancient roots of English, they are different languages and Latin is dead. It gave way to Italian centuries ago. I'm pretty sure the Italians will let you end a sentence with a preposition.

The thing about prepositions in English is that sometimes they belong to our verbs. For example, "to get" has an entirely different meaning from "to get to."

The airport is difficult to get to.

This is a complete sentence. Try to write it without ending with the preposition. You can't. At least, not without writing an entirely different sentence.

The airport is difficult to get.

And "to try" has an entirely different meaning from "to try on."

Try those pants on.

Again, there's no non-awkward way to write this sentence so that it doesn't end with "on." So, some sentences in English simply must end with a preposition in order to present the appropriate meaning without sounding completely convoluted. I have no idea if Latin ever had these kinds of verbs, but we do, so go right ahead.

### 3. *Plural pronouns for one person. When is "they" okay?*

For most of the last, let's say, 50 years, grammar books have said you can't use the pronoun *they* to refer to one person. But for the last 700 years, English speakers have been doing just that. For example,

> When we hire a new employee, they'll need an office.

The *they* in this sentence refers to one new employee, but since we haven't hired said employee yet, we don't know what gender that employee will be. We use this construction all the time with unknown people.

> Does that driver know how to use their turn signal?
> Each person will show up when they are ready.
> Somebody is supposed to be managing the hotel, but they must be on vacation.

These sentences should sound perfectly normal to you, but technically, for a little while, they were wrong. Now, English grammar guides have come to their senses and said, "we were trying to force you to follow a rule for the sake of the rule!" And that's just not how everyday language works.

The great outcome of this change is that it is now grammatically acceptable to use *they/them/their* to refer to a single person, which means people who don't identify as either male or female can also use pronouns that feel more appropriate. Yay inclusion!

4. ***Who/whom. We're not British, so we don't know and almost no one cares.***

English tends to have one word when a person is at the beginning of the sentence (subject) and another word when that person is at the end of the sentence (object).

> I opened the package.
>
> The package was opened by me.

I and me are the same person, but the word is different when it's the subject or the object of the sentence.

| | |
|---|---|
| We | Us |
| He | Him |
| She | Her |
| They | Them |
| Who | Whom |

But English also has some pronouns that don't change:

You You
It It

And now "who" is much closer to you and it than the first group.

If you feel like you definitely need to know when to use "whom," you use it wherever you would use him/them and the m's make it easy to remember. To check, only read the part of the sentence that comes after the place where you want to use who/whom (never the part before). And remember, who/whom are most often used in questions.

**Who/m do you know?**

Do you know *he*? Do you know *him*?

*Him*, so it's *whom*.

Whom do you know?

**Who/m sent you that package?**

Did *they* send you that package? Did *them* send you that package?

*They*, so it's *who*.

Who sent you that package?

Most of the time, the correct answer is *who*. But even when the "correct" answer is *whom*, would you actually say it? And if you did, would you fake a British accent for a second? Probably.

5. ***You can use contractions. They're totally okay as long as you don't forget the apostrophes.***

The rule about contractions was another rule your teachers thought was good for you. But most of our professional writing is actually standing in for spoken conversation we would have with each other. So, yes, you can use contractions when you write, most of the time.

If you're writing something very formal—a report, a legal document—you would probably write out the full words. We still expect these documents to be more proper, more correct, and follow grammar standards. If you are going to wear a suit while you present any part of the document, you probably will not use contractions. If you're going to wear a hoodie while you present any part of the document, you'll def use'm.

Of particular concern when using contractions, though, is that you are actually using them correctly. Remember when we talked about apostrophes? Apostrophes are used in contractions to show that some letters/sounds are being skipped; this is called elision. When you need or want your writing to be grammatically correct, you'll need to read all your contractions as two separate words to make sure you've used the contraction correctly.

For example, to check the previous sentence, I'd (I would) read *you'll* as "you will" and *you've* as "you have."

Extra note: *should've, would've,* and *could've* may sound like they use *of* but they don't. These words are a contraction of *should have, would have,* and *could have.* So, you shouldn't be writing "I should of done that yesterday." If you're being particularly informal, though, you can use "shoulda, woulda, coulda."

*It's* can be especially tricky. *It's* always equals "it is," every single time. Make sure you check it!

It's important to check that its spelling is correct!

Well, that's it. Those are the rules you need to follow and the ones you can ignore.

Do use the oxford comma in your lists, use *'s* to show ownership, spell the words you mean, mean the words you spell, and make all the items in your lists and bullets parallel.

Don't worry about starting sentences with and, ending sentences with on, referring to one person as *they,* asking *whom,* or using contractions.

You are now a grammar master. But consider using one of those services we mentioned back in Chapter III as a backup. Because you should always use protection.

CHAPTER 5

# BE NICE

## But Don't Be a Wuss

You want people to read your messages, feel like they like and trust you, and then do what you say. To be successful in getting people to read your messages, you need to be nice to them. To get them to do what you say, you need to be clear. This section is all about finding the balance between niceness and clarity.

### USE CARE WITH PRONOUNS: I, YOU, WE

Pronouns are noun categories (see how the word *noun* is there inside *pronoun*?). Each one of us is *I* when we are the one speaking. Each one of us is *you* when we are the one listening. So, the *I* and the *you* are categories that help us understand who is speaking and who is listening.

In business writing, we want to use pronouns carefully because they also reveal where our attention is focused. For example, say someone writes a message to you like this:

> I need you to finish the revisions by Friday so I can get the new draft done before next week's meeting. I really want to finish the work this week since I have a lot of things going on next week which will make it hard for me to complete this work on time. Please send me the revisions as soon as you can.

Can you tell where the writer's attention is? Are they focused on their own needs or your needs or the business's needs? Every time we use *I,* we make the main idea of a sentence about ourselves. Sometimes this is necessary. Many times, it's not.

A shortcut is to count the pronouns. The sample above has 4 *I*s and 2 *you*s. And no reference at all to the business as a whole. Unbalanced.

Effective business writing (and business generally) is actually about balancing needs. You need something from me, so I provide it to you and you pay me for it. Balance = happy. This extends to our writing.

Often, a message can be rewritten to focus either on the *you* or on the work itself:

> Would you be able to complete the revisions by Friday? If so, I can revise the new draft for next week's meeting so we can present our best work to the client.

Pronoun count: One *I*, One *you*, One *we*. Balanced.

Also, *we* works best when it represents the *I* and the *you* working together. *We* can also work when you are representing your company, as it extends responsibility beyond you as an individual: *We* care about our customers. Sounds like the whole company values the customers. But when you are using it to represent your company's position, it counts as an *I*: *We* can't help you with that. Sounds like you are just hiding behind the company instead of accepting responsibility for not helping me. SUUUUUUCH a cop-out.

Pronouns frame your relationship with the audience: use them wisely.

## FRAME THE NEGATIVE

No one likes to be the bearer of bad news, but sometimes in business you have to talk about negative things. The key is to bring up unfavorable topics in a careful way. Frame the negative to lessen its impact on your reader's psyche. Here are a couple of ways to do that.

1. Objectively:

   Whenever you have to say negative things, try to take the pronouns (see the section above) out.

   You didn't finish the project.
   The project hasn't been finished yet.

   Your website keeps crashing.
   The website keeps crashing.

By taking out the pronouns, you will appear less like you're attacking your reader and more like you're on the same team dealing with the unfinished project or crashing website.

2. By focusing on the positive potential future:

   Look at the negative and try to flip it to the positive.

   That product is out of stock.
   That product will be in stock soon.

   You missed your flight.
   The next flight leaves in 2 hours.

And a personal favorite from a non-profit's website:

> Our charity reduces illiteracy.

What?! So you make the world a little less bad? Why not just say

> Our charity improves literacy.

Change the reader's attention from what is bad to what could be better in the future. It's like a linguistic credit card: buy now and pay later.

## AVOID SHIT SANDWICHES

A shit sandwich is when you give someone bad news or difficult feedback sandwiched in between two positive remarks. On occasion, when done well, this approach can work. After all, you have to tailor the way you provide feedback to the individual you're speaking or writing to. But often "encouragement" just wastes everyone's time and comes across as shitty. For instance,

> *I really appreciate the way you've been showing up on time to meetings. But I noticed that you missed two deadlines last week. Please call me to discuss. Love those red shoes you wore yesterday!*
>
> "Okay, A-hole."

Fake compliments are patronizing. Even authentic compliments out of place can seem patronizing. So, there's a balance between treating people delicately and treating them like adults. You might come across as harsh if you don't offer encouragement or affirmation, but that depends on the situation.

In business, it conveys more respect for people's time and emotional intelligence to tell them what they need to know up-front, as opposed to giving them a long-winded, sugar-coated shit sandwich. Be kind but direct.

You can always open with a standard greeting like, "I hope your week is off to a nice start." Plus, that's just the way you should probably open any conversation.

Then, try to state the problem in a neutral and objective way: "You missed two deadlines last week." This sentence reports the facts but doesn't have any words that imply judgment.

Follow that with an action statement or question:

> **Statement:** Please make sure to meet the May 21 deadline on the Cornflake project to fulfill our obligation to the client.
>
> **Question:** What is your plan to meet the May 21 deadline on the Cornflake project?

Keep focused on the problem itself and then either instruct the person on how to resolve it or empower them to find their own solutions to resolve it. But do not go off topic and try to hide the fact that there's a problem to resolve. Save any compliments or excitement about weekends and travel plans for other messages.

## ASK THE QUESTION

If you're asking a question, make sure you *ask the question!* Far too many people write "I am wondering if . . ." or "I was wondering . . ." or "I was hoping . . ." Questions presented as statements are a no-no. People have to figure out if there's a question they're supposed to answer. Figuring it out might only take a moment or two, but it's annoying. Your reader might just choose not to answer. This goes back to our point in Chapter II about having a "clear ask." And that will help you not look like a wuss.

> "I was wondering if you'd seen that invoice." – Wuss.
>
> "I was wondering if you'd seen that invoice?" – Super wuss.

That's a question mark on a statement. Definitely not getting that invoice paid . . . at least, not on time.

> "Have you seen the invoice I sent on May 30?" - That's more like it.

## USE PASSIVE VOICE DELIBERATELY

Active and passive voice are called *moods* in grammar books. That's because they tell us how to feel about or interpret events.

> **Active** = I closed the door (I'm performing the action of closing the door)
> **Passive** = The door was closed by me (The door received the action of me closing it)

These two sentences describe the exact same event from two different perspectives. One perspective focuses on what I did; the other focuses on what happened to the door.

Why do we have two ways of talking about the same thing? Because most of the time, English prefers us to say who is doing what. We like action. We like actors. It feels powerful and productive. So, active voice is best most of the time.

However, sometimes, we want to avoid placing blame on others or taking responsibility for something.

> **Placing blame**
> **Active** = You jammed up the copier!

> **More neutral**
> **Passive** = The copier got jammed up!

The first example is mean because it blames someone for the problem. The second example just says what the problem is.

**Taking responsibility**

**Active =** I didn't write down when we were meeting.

**Passive =** Our meeting didn't get written down on my calendar.

The first example is honest but might make us look irresponsible or careless in some circumstances. The second one just says, "Ah, things happen." Shrug. And might be more effective for moving our conversation forward with an audience.

Passive voice should be used sparingly, but purposefully. Use it when you are trying to keep the focus on what happened or off of a specific person. It's especially appropriate for negative situations.

## DON'T USE PASSIVE VOICE TO BE LAZY, AVOIDANT, OR OTHERWISE SLOTH-LIKE

As explained above, passive voice has its function, but don't abuse it. Good writing should still be honest, transparent, clear, and specific. One specific sentence in passive voice among many active sentences is good. Having many passive sentences is bad.

Why? Because passive is boring. It means that no one is doing anything.

> **Example:** The invoice should be sent by Monday. Once it is received, payment will be processed. The check will be sent within 10 days. Once the check is deposited, the invoice will be marked as closed.

Ugh, so much passive voice it sounds like no one is doing anything. Everyone's just waiting for checks and invoices and payments to take care of themselves. This is an office where people spend the day playing bad internet games like team Minesweeper and deliberately avoiding any and all work. Readers experience these passive voice sentences as not only boring but negligent.

> **Revised:** Please send the invoice by Monday. Once it is received, Accounts Payable will process your payment and send a check within 10 days. When the bank notifies us that you've deposited the check, we'll close out the invoice.

Now, one passive voice idea remains: "once it [the check] is received." Every other sentence now has someone—you, Accounts Payable, the bank, we—actively doing work. The only thing we're waiting for (passive voice) is for the invoice to arrive, whether by email or through the post office. This use of passive voice makes sense because it conveys that we have to get this information before further actions occur. And there's nothing you or I can do to make that check get received any sooner.

And now you know exactly what to do that next time someone doesn't answer all three of your very simple questions in your clear and concise email:

> Thanks for responding to only one of the three questions I asked you. You missed the other two. You were probably great at multiple choice tests in college, weren't you, a-hole?

No. Don't write that. Under any circumstances. That example completely violates all the rules we just taught you. Weren't you paying attention?

**"The greatest waste is an unfulfilled idea that fails to connect with audiences, not because it's a bad idea, but because it's not packaged in a way that moves people."**

**- Carmine Gallo,**
***The Storyteller's Secret***

# CONCLUSION

## *You Eloquent Bastard*

At the beginning of this guide, we promised we would help you sound more approachable and competent, give you a clearer sense of priorities, and sharpen your overall business communication skills.

You've learned that writing well matters.

That shorter is almost always better.

That emails have a lot of parts and doing them right is important.

That bots are here to help (that's what they tell us anyway).

That writing has rules, most of which you can break. Except the one about the Oxford comma, because government.

And that there are ways to sound nice and clear at the same time.

That's pretty much all you need to know! These suggestions should ensure the people you work with like you, trust you, and mostly leave you the f%^& alone. So, get back to work and write some good stuff. You can do it. We believe in you.

If it was worth your time to read it, it was worth our time to write it. If it wasn't, write us an angry letter. And make sure to follow all the rules!

# APPENDIX

## Resources

*The Elements of Style,* by William Strunk Jr. and E.B. White. If you have any aspirations to really high-quality prose, this is literally your most important resource. Practically every author in the world considers it a must-have.

*Writing Without Bullshit,* by Josh Bernoff. Think of a 250-page version of our guide. It's a wonderful resource with many more examples and more extensive, detailed, and nonetheless useful information.

Purdue OWL – owl.purdue.edu – the website of Purdue University's Online Writing Lab, which has become famous for giving out free writing advice by real academics. Most useful are the style guides for MLA and APA. If you write reports and need to cite your sources, this is the place to go.

*Eats, Shoots, and Leaves* by Lynne Truss is a hilarious book on grammar. If you don't like grammar and don't want to think about it, this book will not help you at all. If you like grammar—or are grammar-curious—and find humor in spelling or punctuation errors, this book provides a few hours of serious giggles and excellent explanations.

*The Only Grammar Book You'll Ever Need* by Susan Thurman is an adorable little book on grammar for absolutely anyone. It's pretty much the briefest and easiest explanations of everything about English grammar, written in an accessible style that is meant to be a reference. Get a copy. Put it on a shelf near your computer so you can pull it out during Zoom meetings alongside your coffee mug that reads, "I'm silently correcting your grammar."

# ABOUT THE AUTHORS

## JENNY MORSE

Jenny provides business writing training to professionals through her company Appendance, Inc. – appendance.com – which offers corporate seminars and online courses. Her Better Business Writing Pro course won the 2021 Excellence in Communication Consulting award from the Association for Business Communication.

Always focused on achieving big goals, she's designed her own personal marathon; ghostwritten for CEOs; published poems, articles, and a monthly blog; and successfully managed to feed an orchid two ice cubes a week since 2020.

Jenny loves that she is living her childhood dream of getting paid to read, since she gets to help others understand the rules and reasons of language in whatever context might be needed. Her career in writing and teaching has led her through three degrees, all fifty states, and five continents—and she looks forward to seeing where it might take her next.

## JOHN GARVEY

John is an author, illustrator, business writing coach, and marketing copywriter. The Chief Storytelling Officer at Garvington Creative, John helps purpose-driven businesses connect with high-value clients through creative writing, humor, and clear strategic messaging.

As the Chief Creative Whatchamacallit at Creative Follies — creativefollies.com — John is The World's Most Prodigious and Sought-After T-Rex Unicycling Artist. In this capacity, he wrote and illustrated the children's book, *A T-Rex Shouldn't Ride a Unicycle,* with more publications on the way. His art appears on tee-shirts and coffee mugs in various living rooms and offices (shouldn't yours be one of them?).

John has written for dozens of lifestyle magazines, company blogs, and business publications. Writing has always been one of the key ingredients for keeping his sanity, and he's good at it by virtue of having done a lot of it.

www.ingramcontent.com/pod-product-compliance
Lightning Source LLC
LaVergne TN
LVHW050541100826
845148LV00002B/647